The Constitution of
The State of North Carolina:
A Quick Reference Guide

Bootblack Budget Books
Copyright 2018 ©
ISBN-13: 978-1720330318
ISBN-10: 172033031X

Contents:

Preamble – Page 20

ARTICLE I: DECLARATION OF RIGHTS – Page 21

Section 1. The Equality and Rights of Persons

Section 2. Sovereignty of the People

Section 3. Internal Government of the State

Section 4. Secession Prohibited

Section 5. Allegiance to the United States

Section 6. Separation of powers

Section 7. Suspending Laws

Section 8. Representation and Taxation

Section 9. Frequent Elections

Section 10. Free Elections

Section 11. Property Qualifications

Section 12. Right of Assembly and Petition

Section 13. Religious Liberty

Section 14. Freedom of Speech and Press

Section 15. Education

Section 16. Ex Post Facto Laws

Section 17. Slavery and Involuntary Servitude

Section 18. Court Shall be Open

Section 19. Law of the Land; Equal Protection of the Laws

Section 20. General Warrants

Section 21. Inquiry into restraints on Liberty

Section 22. Modes of Prosecution

Section 23. Rights of Accused

Section 24. Right of Jury Trial in Criminal Cases

Section 25. Right of Jury Trial in Civil Cases

Section 26. Jury Service

Section 27. Bail, Fines, and Punishments

Section 28. Imprisonment for Debt

Section 29. Treason Against the State

Section 30. Militia and the Right to Bear Arms

Section 31. Quartering of Soldiers

Section 32. Exclusive Emoluments

Section 33. Hereditary Emoluments and Honors

Section 34. Perpetuities and Monopolies

Section 35. Recurrence to Fundamental Principles

Section 36. Other Rights of the People

Section 37. Rights of Victims of Crime

ARTICLE II: LEGISLATIVE – Page 30

Section 1. Legislative Power

Section 2. Number of Senators

Section 3. Senate Districts; Apportionment of Senators

Section 4. Number of Representatives

Section 5. Representative Districts; Apportionment of Representatives

Section 6. Qualifications for Senator

Section 7. Qualifications for Representative

Section 8. Elections

Section 9. Term of Office

Section 10. Vacancies

Section 11. Sessions

Section 12. Oath of Members

Section 13. President of the Senate

Section 14. Other Officers of the Senate

Section 15. Officers of the House of Representatives

Section 16. Compensation and Allowances

Section 17. Journals

Section 18. Protests

Section 19. Record Votes

Section 20. Powers of the General Assembly

Section 21. Style of the Acts

Section 22. Action on Bills

Section 23. Revenue Bills

Section 24. Limitations on Local, Private, and Special Legislation

ARTICLE III: EXECUTIVE – Page 41

Section 1. Executive Power

Section 2. Governor and Lieutenant Governor: Election, Term, and Qualifications

Section 3. Succession to Office of Governor

Section 4. Oath of Office for Governor

Section 5. Duties of Governor

Section 6. Duties of the Lieutenant Governor

Section 7. Other Elective Officers

Section 8. Council of State

Section 9. Compensation and Allowances

Section 10. Seal of State

Section 11. Administrative Departments

ARTICLE IV: JUDICIAL – Page 50

Section 1. Judicial Power

Section 2. General Court of Justice

Section 3. Judicial Powers of Administrative Agencies

Section 4. Court for the Trial of Impeachments

Section 5. Appellate Division

Section 6. Supreme Court

Section 7. Court of Appeals

Section 8. Retirement of Justices and Judges

Section 9. Superior Courts shall be held annually in each county.

Section 10. District Courts

Section 11. Assignment of Judges

Section 12. Jurisdiction of the General Court of Justice

Section 13. Forms of action; rules of procedure

(1) FORMS OF ACTION

Section 14. Waiver of Jury Trial

Section 15. Administration

Section 16. Terms of Office and Election of Justices of the Supreme Court, Judges of the Court of Appeals, and Judges of the Superior Court

Section 17. Removal of Judges, Magistrates and Clerks

Section 18. District Attorney and Prosecutorial Districts

Section 19. Vacancies

Section 20. Revenues and Expenses of the Judicial Department

Section 21. Fees, Salaries, and Emoluments

Section 22. Qualification of Justices and Judges

ARTICLE V: FINANCE – Page 60

Section 1. No Capitation Tax to be Levied

Section 2. State and Local Taxation

Section 3. Limitations Upon The Increase of State Debt

Section 4. Limitations Upon the Increase of Local Government Debt

Section 5. Acts Levying Taxes to State Objects

Section 6. Inviolability of Sinking Funds and Retirement Funds

Section 7. Drawing Public Money

Section 8. Health Care Facilities

Section 9. Capital Projects for Industry

Section 10. Joint Ownership of Generation and Transmission Facilities

Section 11. Capital Projects for Agriculture

Section 12. Higher Education Facilities

Section 13. Seaport and Airport Facilities

Section 14. Project Development Financing

ARTICLE VI: SUFFRAGE AND ELIGIBILITY TO OFFICE – Page 73

Section 1. Who May Vote

Section 2. Qualifications of Voter

Section 3. Registration

Section 4. Qualification for Registration

Section 5. Elections by People and General Assembly

Section 6. Eligibility to Elective Office

Section 7. Oath

Section 8. Disqualifications for Office

Section 9. Dual Office Holding

Section 10. Continuation in Office

ARTICLE VII: LOCAL GOVERNMENT – Page 77

Section 1. General Assembly to Provide for Local Government

Section 2. Sheriffs

Section 3. Merged or Consolidated Counties

ARTICLE VIII: CORPORATIONS – Page 79

Section 1. Corporate Charters

Section 2. Corporations Defined

ARTICLE IX: EDUCATION – Page 80

Section 1. Education Encouraged

Section 2. Uniform System of Schools

Section 3. School Attendance

Section 4. State Board of Education

Section 5. Powers and Duties of Board

Section 6. State School Fund

Section 7. County School Fund; State Fund for Certain Moneys

Section 8. Higher Education

Section 9. Benefits of Public Institutions of Higher Education

Section 10. Escheats

ARTICLE X: HOMESTEADS AND EXEMPTIONS – Page 84

Section 1. Personal Property Exemptions

Section 2. Homestead Exemptions

Section 3. Mechanics And Laborers Liens

Section 4. Property of Married Women Secured to Them

Section 5. Insurance

ARTICLE XI: PUNISHMENTS, CORRECTIONS, AND CHARITIES – Page 87

Section 1. Punishments

Section 2. Death Punishment

Section 3. Charitable and Correctional Institutions and Agencies

Section 4. Welfare Policy; Board of Public Welfare

ARTICLE XII: MILITARY FORCES – Page 88

Section 1. Governor is Commander in Chief

ARTICLE XIII: CONVENTIONS; CONSTITUTIONAL AMENDMENT AND REVISION – Page 89

Section 1. Convention of the People

Section 2. Power to Revise or Amend Constitution Reserved to People

Section 3. Revision or Amendment by Convention of the People

Section 4. Revision or Amendment by Legislative Initiation

ARTICLE XIV: MISCELLANEOUS – Page 91

Section 1. Seat of Government

Section 2. State Boundaries

Section 3. General Laws Defined

Section 4. Continuity of Laws; Protection of Office Holders

Section 5. Conservation of Natural Resources

Section 6. Marriage

PREAMBLE

We, the people of the State of North Carolina, grateful to Almighty God, the Sovereign Ruler of Nations, for the preservation of the American Union and the existence of our civil, political and religious liberties, and acknowledging our dependence upon Him for the continuance of those blessings to us and our posterity, do, for the more certain security thereof and for the better government of this State, ordain and establish this Constitution.

ARTICLE I: DECLARATION OF RIGHTS

That the great, general, and essential principles of liberty and free government may be recognized and established, and that the relations of this State to the Union and government of the United States and those of the people of this State to the rest of the American people may be defined and affirmed, we do declare that:

Section 1. The Equality and Rights of Persons

We hold it to be self-evident that all persons are created equal; that they are endowed by their Creator with certain inalienable rights; that among these are life, liberty, the enjoyment of the fruits of their own labor, and the pursuit of happiness.

Section 2. Sovereignty of the People

All political power is vested in and derived from the people; all government of right originates from the people, is founded upon their will only, and is instituted solely for the good of the whole.

Section 3. Internal Government of the State

The people of this State have the inherent, sole, and exclusive right of regulating the internal government and police thereof, and of altering or abolishing their Constitution and form of government whenever it may be necessary to their safety and happiness; but every such right shall be exercised in pursuance of law and consistently with the Constitution of the United States.

Section 4. Secession Prohibited

This State shall ever remain a member of the American Union; the people thereof are part of the American nation; there is no right on the part of this State to secede; and all attempts, from whatever source or upon whatever pretext, to dissolve this Union or to sever this Nation, shall be resisted with the whole power of the State.

Section 5. Allegiance to the United States

Every citizen of this State owes paramount allegiance to the Constitution and government of the United States, and no law or ordinance of the State in contravention or subversion thereof can have any binding force.

Section 6. Separation of powers

The legislative, executive, and supreme judicial powers of the State government shall be forever separate and distinct from each other.

Section 7. Suspending Laws

All power of suspending laws or the execution of laws by any authority, without the consent of the representatives of the people, is injurious to their rights and shall not be exercised.

Section 8. Representation and Taxation

The people of this State shall not be taxed or made subject to the payment of any impost or duty without the consent of themselves or their representatives in the General Assembly, freely given.

Section 9. Frequent Elections

For redress of grievances and for amending and strengthening the laws, elections shall be often held.

Section 10. Free Elections

All elections shall be free.

Section 11. Property Qualifications

As political rights and privileges are not dependent upon or modified by property, no property qualification shall affect the right to vote or hold office.

Section 12. Right of Assembly and Petition

The people have a right to assemble together to consult for their common good, to instruct their representatives, and to apply to the General Assembly for redress of grievances; but secret political societies are dangerous to the liberties of a free people and shall not be tolerated.

Section 13. Religious Liberty

All persons have a natural and inalienable right to worship Almighty God according to the dictates of their own consciences, and no human authority shall, in any case whatever, control or interfere with the rights of conscience.

Section 14. Freedom of Speech and Press

Freedom of speech and of the press are two of the great bulwarks of liberty and therefore shall never be restrained, but every person shall be held responsible for their abuse.

Section 15. Education

The people have a right to the privilege of education, and it is the duty of the State to guard and maintain that right.

Section 16. Ex Post Facto Laws

Retrospective laws, punishing acts committed before the existence of such laws and by them only declared criminal, are oppressive, unjust, and incompatible with liberty, and therefore no ex post facto law shall be enacted. No law taxing retrospectively sales, purchases, or other acts previously done shall be enacted.

Section 17. Slavery and Involuntary Servitude

Slavery is forever prohibited. Involuntary servitude, except as a punishment for crime whereof the parties have been adjudged guilty, is forever prohibited.

Section 18. Court Shall be Open

All courts shall be open; every person for an injury done him in his lands, goods, person, or reputation shall have remedy by due course of law; and right and justice shall be administered without favor, denial, or delay.

Section 19. Law of the Land; Equal Protection of the Laws

No person shall be taken, imprisoned, or disseized of his freehold, liberties, or privileges, or outlawed, or exiled, or in any manner deprived of his life, liberty, or property, but by the law of the land. No person shall be denied the equal protection of the laws; nor shall any person be subjected to discrimination by the State because of race, color, religion, or national origin.

Section 20. General Warrants

General warrants, whereby any officer or other person may be commanded to search suspected places without evidence of the act committed, or to seize any person or persons not named, whose offense is not particularly described and supported by evidence, are dangerous to liberty and shall not be granted.

Section 21. Inquiry into restraints on Liberty

Every person restrained of his liberty is entitled to a remedy to inquire into the lawfulness thereof, and to remove the restraint if unlawful, and that remedy shall not be denied or delayed. The privilege of the writ of habeas corpus shall not be suspended.

Section 22. Modes of Prosecution

Except in misdemeanor cases initiated in the District Court Division, no person shall be put to answer any criminal charge but by indictment, presentment, or impeachment. But any person, when represented by counsel, may, under such regulations as the General Assembly shall prescribe, waive indictment in noncapital cases.

Section 23. Rights of Accused

In all criminal prosecutions, every person charged with crime has the right to be informed of the accusation and to confront the accusers and witnesses with other testimony, and to have counsel for defense, and not be compelled to give self-incriminating evidence, or to pay costs, jail fees, or necessary witness fees of the defense, unless found guilty.

Section 24. Right of Jury Trial in Criminal Cases

No person shall be convicted of any crime but by the unanimous verdict of a jury in open court, except that a person accused of any criminal offense for which the State is not seeking a sentence of death in superior court may, in writing or on the record in the court and with the consent of the trial judge, waive jury trial, subject to procedures prescribed by the General Assembly. The General Assembly may, however, provide for other means of trial for misdemeanors, with the right of appeal for trial de novo.

Section 25. Right of Jury Trial in Civil Cases

In all controversies at law respecting property, the ancient mode of trial by jury is one of the best securities of the rights of the people, and shall remain sacred and inviolable.

Section 26. Jury Service

No person shall be excluded from jury service on account of sex, race, color, religion, or national origin.

Section 27. Bail, Fines, and Punishments

Excessive bail shall not be required, nor excessive fines imposed, nor cruel or unusual punishments inflicted.

Section 28. Imprisonment for Debt

There shall be no imprisonment for debt in this State, except in cases of fraud.

Section 29. Treason Against the State

Treason against the State shall consist only of levying war against it or adhering to its enemies by giving them aid and comfort. No person shall be convicted of treason unless on the testimony of two witnesses to the same overt act, or on confession in open court. No conviction of treason or attainder shall work corruption of blood or forfeiture.

Section 30. Militia and the Right to Bear Arms

A well regulated militia being necessary to the security of a free State, the right of the people to keep and bear arms shall not be infringed; and, as standing armies in time of peace are dangerous to liberty, they shall not be maintained, and the military shall be kept under strict subordination to, and governed by, the civil power. Nothing herein shall justify the practice of carrying concealed weapons, or prevent the General Assembly from enacting penal statutes against that practice.

Section 31. Quartering of Soldiers

No soldier shall in time of peace be quartered in any house without the consent of the owner, nor in time of war but in a manner prescribed by law.

Section 32. Exclusive Emoluments

No person or set of persons is entitled to exclusive or separate emoluments or privileges from the community but in consideration of public services.

Section 33. Hereditary Emoluments and Honors

No hereditary emoluments, privileges, or honors shall be granted or conferred in this State.

Section 34. Perpetuities and Monopolies

Perpetuities and monopolies are contrary to the genius of a free state and shall not be allowed.

Section 35. Recurrence to Fundamental Principles

A frequent recurrence to fundamental principles is absolutely necessary to preserve the blessings of liberty.

Section 36. Other Rights of the People

The enumeration of rights in this Article shall not be construed to impair or deny others retained by the people.

Section 37. Rights of Victims of Crime

(1) BASIC RIGHTS

Victims of crime, as prescribed by law, shall be entitled to the following basic rights:

(a) The right as prescribed by law to be informed of and to be present at court proceedings of the accused.

(b) The right to be heard at sentencing of the accused in a manner prescribed by law, and at other times as prescribed by law or deemed appropriate by the court.

(c) The right as prescribed by law to receive restitution.

(d) The right as prescribed by law to be given information about the crime, how the criminal justice system works, the rights of victims, and the availability of services for victims.

(e) The right as prescribed by law to receive information about the conviction or final disposition and sentence of the accused.

(f) The right as prescribed by law to receive notification of escape, release, proposed parole or pardon of the accused, or notice of a reprieve or commutation of the accused's sentence.

(g) The right as prescribed by law to present their views and concerns to the Governor or agency considering any action that could result in the release of the accused, prior to such action becoming effective.

(h) The right as prescribed by law to confer with the prosecution.

(2) NO MONEY DAMAGES; OTHER ENFORCEMENT

Nothing in this section shall be construed as creating a claim for money damages against the State, a county, a municipality, or any of the agencies, instrumentalities, or employees thereof. The General Assembly may provide for other remedies to ensure adequate enforcement of this section.

(3) NO GROUND FOR RELIEF IN CRIMINAL CASE

The failure or inability of any person to provide a right or service provided under this section may not be used by a defendant in a criminal case, an inmate, or any other accused as a ground for relief in any trial, appeal, postconviction litigation, habeas corpus, civil action, or any similar criminal or civil proceeding.

ARTICLE II: LEGISLATIVE

Section 1. Legislative Power

The legislative power of the State shall be vested in the General Assembly, which shall consist of a Senate and a House of Representatives.

Section 2. Number of Senators

The Senate shall be composed of 50 Senators, biennially chosen by ballot.

Section 3. Senate Districts; Apportionment of Senators

The Senators shall be elected from districts. The General Assembly, at the first regular session convening after the return of every decennial census of population taken by order of Congress, shall revise the senate districts and the apportionment of Senators among those districts, subject to the following requirements:

(1) Each Senator shall represent, as nearly as may be, an equal number of inhabitants, the number of inhabitants that each Senator represents being determined for this purpose by dividing the population of the district that he represents by the number of Senators apportioned to that district;

(2) Each senate district shall at all times consist of contiguous territory;

(3) No county shall be divided in the formation of a senate district;

(4) When established, the senate districts and the apportionment of Senators shall remain unaltered until the return of another decennial census of population taken by order of Congress.

Section 4. Number of Representatives

The House of Representatives shall be composed of 120 Representatives, biennially chosen by ballot.

Section 5. Representative Districts; Apportionment of Representatives

The Representatives shall be elected from districts. The General Assembly, at the first regular session convening after the return of every decennial census of population taken by order of Congress, shall revise the representative districts and the apportionment of Representatives among those districts, subject to the following requirements:

(1) Each Representative shall represent, as nearly as may be, an equal number of inhabitants, the number of inhabitants that each Representative represents being determined for this purpose by dividing the population of the district that he represents by the number of Representatives apportioned to that district;

(2) Each representative district shall at all times consist of contiguous territory;

(3) No county shall be divided in the formation of a representative district;

(4) When established, the representative districts and the apportionment of Representatives shall remain unaltered until the return of another decennial census of population taken by order of Congress.

Section 6. Qualifications for Senator

Each Senator, at the time of his election, shall be not less than 25 years of age, shall be a qualified voter of the State, and shall have resided in the State as a citizen for two years and in the district for which he is chosen for one year immediately preceding his election.

Section 7. Qualifications for Representative

Each Representative, at the time of his election, shall be a qualified voter of the State, and shall have resided in the district for which he is chosen for one year immediately preceding his election.

Section 8. Elections

The election for members of the General Assembly shall be held for the respective districts in 1972 and every two years thereafter, at the places and on the day prescribed by law.

Section 9. Term of Office

The term of office of Senators and Representatives shall commence on the first day of January next after their election.

Section 10. Vacancies

Every vacancy occurring in the membership of the General Assembly by reason of death, resignation, or other cause shall be filled in the manner prescribed by law.

Section 11. Sessions

(1) REGULAR SESSIONS

The General Assembly shall meet in regular session in 1973 and every two years thereafter on the day prescribed by law. Neither house shall proceed upon public business unless a majority of all of its members are actually present.

(2) EXTRA SESSIONS ON LEGISLATIVE CALL

The President of the Senate and the Speaker of the House of Representatives shall convene the General Assembly in extra session by their joint proclamation upon receipt by the President of the Senate of written requests therefor signed by three-fifths of all the members of the Senate and upon receipt by the Speaker of the House of Representatives of written requests therefor signed by three-fifths of all the members of the House of Representatives.

Section 12. Oath of Members

Each member of the General Assembly, before taking his seat, shall take an oath or affirmation that he will support the Constitution and laws of the United States and the Constitution of the State of North Carolina, and will faithfully discharge his duty as a member of the Senate or House of Representatives.

Section 13. President of the Senate

The Lieutenant Governor shall be President of the Senate and shall preside over the Senate, but shall have no vote unless the Senate is equally divided.

Section 14. Other Officers of the Senate

(1) PRESIDENT PRO TEMPORE - SUCCESSION TO PRESIDENCY

The Senate shall elect from its membership a President Pro Tempore, who shall become President of the Senate upon the failure of the Lieutenant Governor-elect to qualify, or upon succession by the Lieutenant Governor to the office of Governor, or upon the death, resignation, or removal from office of the President of the Senate, and who shall serve until the expiration of his term of office as Senator.

(2) PRESIDENT PRO TEMPORE - TEMPORARY SUCCESSION

During the physical or mental incapacity of the President of the Senate to perform the duties of his office, or during the absence of the President of the Senate, the President Pro Tempore shall preside over the Senate.

(3) OTHER OFFICERS

The Senate shall elect its other officers.

Section 15. Officers of the House of Representatives

The House of Representatives shall elect its Speaker and other officers.

Section 16. Compensation and Allowances

The members and officers of the General Assembly shall receive for their services the compensation and allowances prescribed by law. An increase in the compensation or allowances of members shall become effective at the beginning of the next regular session of the General Assembly following the session at which it was enacted.

Section 17. Journals

Each house shall keep a journal of its proceedings, which shall be printed and made public immediately after the adjournment of the General Assembly.

Section 18. Protests

Any member of either house may dissent from and protest against any act or resolve which he may think injurious to the public or to any individual, and have the reasons of his dissent entered on the journal.

Section 19. Record Votes

Upon motion made in either house and seconded by one fifth of the members present, the yeas and nays upon any question shall be taken and entered upon the journal.

Section 20. Powers of the General Assembly

Each house shall be judge of the qualifications and elections of its own members, shall sit upon its own adjournment from day to day, and shall prepare bills to be enacted into laws. The two houses may jointly adjourn to any future day or other place. Either house may, of its own motion, adjourn for a period not in excess of three days.

Section 21. Style of the Acts

The style of the acts shall be: "The General Assembly of North Carolina enacts:".

Section 22. Action on Bills

(1) BILLS SUBJECT TO VETO BY GOVERNOR; OVERRIDE OF VETO

Except as provided by subsections (2) through (6) of this section, all bills shall be read three times in each house and shall be signed by the presiding officer of each house before being presented to the Governor. If the Governor approves, the Governor shall sign it and it shall become a law; but if not, the Governor shall return it with objections, together with a veto message stating the reasons for such objections, to that house in which it shall have originated, which shall enter the objections and veto message at large on its journal, and proceed to reconsider it. If after such reconsideration three-fifths of the members of that house present and voting shall agree to pass the bill, it shall be sent, together with the objections and veto message, to the other house, by which it shall likewise be reconsidered; and if approved by three-fifths of the members of that house present and voting, it shall become a law notwithstanding the objections of the Governor. In all such cases the votes of both houses shall be determined by yeas and nays, and the names of the members voting shall be entered on the journal of each house respectively.

(2) AMENDMENTS TO CONSTITUTION OF NORTH CAROLINA

Every bill proposing a new or revised Constitution or an amendment or amendments to this Constitution or calling a convention of the people of this State, and containing no other matter, shall be submitted to the qualified voters of this State after it shall have been read three times in each house and signed by the presiding officers of both houses.

(3) AMENDMENTS TO CONSTITUTION OF THE UNITED STATES

Every bill approving an amendment to the Constitution of the United States, or applying for a convention to propose amendments to the Constitution of the United States, and containing no other matter, shall be read three times in each house before it becomes law, and shall be signed by the presiding officers of both houses.

(4) JOINT RESOLUTIONS

Every joint resolution shall be read three times in each house before it becomes effective and shall be signed by the presiding officers of both houses.

(5) OTHER EXCEPTIONS. EVERY BILL:

(a) In which the General Assembly makes an appointment or appointments to public office and which contains no other matter;

(b) Revising the senate districts and the apportionment of Senators among those districts and containing no other matter;

(c) Revising the representative districts and the apportionment of Representatives among those districts and containing no other matter; or

(d) Revising the districts for the election of members of the House of Representatives of the Congress of the United States and the apportionment of Representatives among those districts and containing no other matter,
shall be read three times in each house before it becomes law and shall be signed by the presiding officers of both houses.

(6) LOCAL BILLS

Every bill that applies in fewer than 15 counties shall be read three times in each house before it becomes law and shall be signed by the presiding officers of both houses. The exemption from veto by the Governor provided in this subsection does not apply if the bill, at the time it is signed by the presiding officers:

(a) Would extend the application of a law signed by the presiding officers during that two year term of the General Assembly so that the law would apply in more than half the counties in the State, or

(b) Would enact a law identical in effect to another law or laws signed by the presiding officers during that two year term of the General Assembly that the result of those laws taken together would be a law applying in more than half the counties in the State.

Notwithstanding any other language in this subsection, the exemption from veto provided by this subsection does not apply to any bill to enact a general law classified by population or other criteria, or to any bill that contains an appropriation from the State treasury.

(7) TIME FOR ACTION BY GOVERNOR; RECONVENING OF SESSION

If any bill shall not be returned by the Governor within 10 days after it shall have been presented to him, the same shall be a law in like manner as if he had signed it, unless the General Assembly shall have adjourned:

(a) For more than 30 days jointly as provided under Section 20 of Article II of this Constitution; or

(b) Sine die in which case it shall become a law unless, within 30 days after such adjournment, it is returned by the Governor with objections and veto message to that house in which it shall have originated. When the General Assembly has adjourned sine die or for more than 30 days jointly as provided under Section 20 of Article II of this Constitution, the Governor shall reconvene that session as provided by Section 5(11) of Article III of this Constitution for reconsideration of the bill, and if the Governor does not reconvene the session, the bill shall become law on the fortieth day after such adjournment. Notwithstanding the previous sentence, if the Governor prior to reconvening the session receives written requests dated no earlier than 30 days after such adjournment, signed by a majority of the members of each house that a reconvened session to reconsider vetoed legislation is unnecessary, the Governor shall not reconvene the session for that purpose and any legislation vetoed in accordance with this section after adjournment shall not become law.

(8) RETURN OF BILLS AFTER ADJOURNMENT

For purposes of return of bills not approved by the Governor, each house shall designate an officer to receive returned bills during its adjournment.

Section 23. Revenue Bills

No law shall be enacted to raise money on the credit of the State, or to pledge the faith of the State directly or indirectly for the payment of any debt, or to impose any tax upon the people of the State, or to allow the counties, cities, or towns to do so, unless the bill for the purpose shall have been read three several times in each house of the General Assembly and passed three several readings, which readings shall have been on three different days, and shall have been agreed to by each house respectively, and unless the yeas and nays on the second and third readings of the bill shall have been entered on the journal.

Section 24. Limitations on Local, Private, and Special Legislation

(1) PROHIBITED SUBJECTS

The General Assembly shall not enact any local, private, or special act or resolution:

(a) Relating to health, sanitation, and the abatement of nuisances;

(b) Changing the names of cities, towns, and townships;

(c) Authorizing the laying out, opening, altering, maintaining, or discontinuing of highways, streets, or alleys;

(d) Relating to ferries or bridges;

(e) Relating to non-navigable streams;

(f) Relating to cemeteries;

(g) Relating to the pay of jurors;

(h) Erecting new townships, or changing township lines, or establishing or changing the lines of school districts;

(i) Remitting fines, penalties, and forfeitures, or refunding moneys legally paid into the public treasury;

(j) Regulating labor, trade, mining, or manufacturing;

(k) Extending the time for the levy or collection of taxes or otherwise relieving any collector of taxes from the due performance of his official duties or his sureties from liability;

(l) Giving effect to informal wills and deeds;

(m) Granting a divorce or securing alimony in any individual case;

(n) Altering the name of any person, or legitimating any person not born in lawful wedlock, or restoring to the rights of citizenship any person convicted of a felony.

(2) REPEALS

Nor shall the General Assembly enact any such local, private, or special act by the partial repeal of a general law; but the General Assembly may at any time repeal local, private, or special laws enacted by it.

(3) PROHIBITED ACTS VOID

Any local, private, or special act or resolution enacted in violation of the provisions of this Section shall be void.

(4) GENERAL LAWS

The General Assembly may enact general laws regulating the matters set out in this Section.

ARTICLE III: EXECUTIVE

Section 1. Executive Power

The executive power of the State shall be vested in the Governor.

Section 2. Governor and Lieutenant Governor: Election, Term, and Qualifications

(1) ELECTION AND TERM

The Governor and Lieutenant Governor shall be elected by the qualified voters of the State in 1972 and every four years thereafter, at the same time and places as members of the General Assembly are elected. Their term of office shall be four years and shall commence on the first day of January next after their election and continue until their successors are elected and qualified.

(2) QUALIFICATIONS

No person shall be eligible for election to the office of Governor or Lieutenant Governor unless, at the time of his election, he shall have attained the age of 30 years and shall have been a citizen of the United States for five years and a resident of this State for two years immediately preceding his election. No person elected to the office of Governor or Lieutenant Governor shall be eligible for election to more than two consecutive terms of the same office.

Section 3. Succession to Office of Governor

(1) SUCCESSION AS GOVERNOR

The Lieutenant Governor-elect shall become Governor upon the failure of the Governor-elect to qualify. The Lieutenant Governor shall become Governor upon the death, resignation, or removal from office of the Governor. The further order of succession to the office of Governor shall be prescribed by law. A successor shall serve for the remainder of the term of the Governor whom he succeeds and until a new Governor is elected and qualified.

(2) SUCCESSION AS ACTING GOVERNOR

During the absence of the Governor from the State, or during the physical or mental incapacity of the Governor to perform the duties of his office, the Lieutenant Governor shall be Acting Governor. The further order of succession as Acting Governor shall be prescribed by law.

(3) PHYSICAL INCAPACITY

The Governor may, by a written statement filed with the Attorney General, declare that he is physically incapable of performing the duties of his office, and may thereafter in the same manner declare that he is physically capable of performing the duties of his office.

(4) MENTAL INCAPACITY

The mental incapacity of the Governor to perform the duties of his office shall be determined only by joint resolution adopted by a vote of two-thirds of all the members of each house of the General Assembly. Thereafter, the mental capacity of the Governor to perform the duties of his office shall be determined only by joint resolution adopted by a vote of a majority of all the members of each house of the General Assembly. In all cases, the General Assembly shall give the Governor such notice as it may deem proper and shall allow him an opportunity to be heard before a joint session of the General Assembly before it takes final action. When the General Assembly is not in session, the Council of State, a majority of its members concurring, may convene it in extra session for the purpose of proceeding under this paragraph.

(5) IMPEACHMENT

Removal of the Governor from office for any other cause shall be by impeachment.

Section 4. Oath of Office for Governor

The Governor, before entering upon the duties of his office, shall, before any Justice of the Supreme Court, take an oath or affirmation that he will support the Constitution and laws of the United States and of the State of North Carolina, and that he will faithfully perform the duties pertaining to the office of governor.

Section 5. Duties of Governor

(1) RESIDENCE

The Governor shall reside at the seat of government of this State.

(2) INFORMATION TO GENERAL ASSEMBLY

The Governor shall from time to time give the General Assembly information of the affairs of the State and recommend to their consideration such measures as he shall deem expedient.

(3) BUDGET

The Governor shall prepare and recommend to the General Assembly a comprehensive budget of the anticipated revenue and proposed expenditures of the State for the ensuing fiscal period. The budget as enacted by the General Assembly shall be administered by the Governor.

The total expenditures of the State for the fiscal period covered by the budget shall not exceed the total of receipts during that fiscal period and the surplus remaining in the State Treasury at the beginning of the period. To insure that the State does not incur a deficit for any fiscal period, the Governor shall continually survey the collection of the revenue and shall effect the necessary economies in State expenditures, after first making adequate provision for the prompt payment of the principal of and interest on bonds and notes of the State according to their terms, whenever he determines that receipts during the fiscal period, when added to any surplus remaining in the State Treasury at the beginning of the period, will not be sufficient to meet budgeted expenditures. This section shall not be construed to impair the power of the State to issue its bonds and notes within the limitations imposed in Article V of this Constitution, nor to impair the obligation of bonds and notes of the State now outstanding or issued hereafter.

(4) EXECUTION OF LAWS

The Governor shall take care that the laws be faithfully executed.

(5) COMMANDER IN CHIEF

The Governor shall be Commander in Chief of the military forces of the State except when they shall be called into the service of the United States.

(6) CLEMENCY

The Governor may grant reprieves, commutations, and pardons, after conviction, for all offenses (except in cases of impeachment), upon such conditions as he may think proper, subject to regulations prescribed by law relative to the manner of applying for pardons. The terms reprieves, commutations, and pardons shall not include paroles.

(7) EXTRA SESSIONS

The Governor may, on extraordinary occasions, by and with the advice of the Council of State, convene the General Assembly in extra session by his proclamation, stating therein the purpose or purposes for which they are thus convened.

(8) APPOINTMENTS

The Governor shall nominate and by and with the advice and consent of a majority of the Senators appoint all officers whose appointments are not otherwise provided for.

(9) INFORMATION

The Governor may at any time require information in writing from the head of any administrative department or agency upon any subject relating to the duties of his office.

(10) ADMINISTRATIVE REORGANIZATION

The General Assembly shall prescribe the functions, powers, and duties of the administrative departments and agencies of the State and may alter them from time to time, but the Governor may make such changes in the allocation of offices and agencies and in the allocation of those functions, powers, and duties as he considers necessary for efficient administration. If those changes affect existing law, they shall be set forth in executive orders, which shall be submitted to the General Assembly not later than the sixtieth calendar day of its session, and shall become effective and shall have the force of law upon adjournment sine die of the session, unless specifically disapproved by resolution of either house of the General Assembly or specifically modified by joint resolution of both houses of the General Assembly.

(11) RECONVENED SESSIONS

The Governor shall, when required by Section 22 of Article II of this Constitution, reconvene a session of the General Assembly. At such reconvened session, the General Assembly may only consider such bills as were returned by the Governor to that reconvened session for reconsideration. Such reconvened session shall begin on a date set by the Governor, but no later than 40 days after the General Assembly adjourned:

(a) For more than 30 days jointly as provided under Section 20 of Article II of this Constitution; or

(b) Sine die. If the date of reconvening the session occurs after the expiration of the terms of office of the members of the General Assembly, then the members serving for the reconvened session shall be the members for the succeeding term.

Section 6. Duties of the Lieutenant Governor

The Lieutenant Governor shall be President of the Senate, but shall have no vote unless the Senate is equally divided. He shall perform such additional duties as the General Assembly or the Governor may assign to him. He shall receive the compensation and allowances prescribed by law.

Section 7. Other Elective Officers

(1) OFFICERS

A Secretary of State, an Auditor, a Treasurer, a Superintendent of Public Instruction, an Attorney General, a Commissioner of Agriculture, a Commissioner of Labor, and a Commissioner of Insurance shall be elected by the qualified voters of the State in 1972 and every four years thereafter, at the same time and places as members of the General Assembly are elected. Their term of office shall be four years and shall commence on the first day of January next after their election and continue until their successors are elected and qualified.

(2) DUTIES

Their respective duties shall be prescribed by law.

(3) VACANCIES

If the office of any of these officers is vacated by death, resignation, or otherwise, it shall be the duty of the Governor to appoint another to serve until his successor is elected and qualified. Every such vacancy shall be filled by election at the first election for members of the General Assembly that occurs more than 60 days after the vacancy has taken place, and the person chosen shall hold the office for the remainder of the unexpired term fixed in this Section. When a vacancy occurs in the office of any of the officers named in this Section and the term expires on the first day of January succeeding the next election for members of the General Assembly, the Governor shall appoint to fill the vacancy for the unexpired term of the office.

(4) INTERIM OFFICERS

Upon the occurrence of a vacancy in the office of any one of these officers for any of the causes stated in the preceding paragraph, the Governor may appoint an interim officer to perform the duties of that office until a person is appointed or elected pursuant to this Section to fill the vacancy and is qualified.

(5) ACTING OFFICERS

During the physical or mental incapacity of any one of these officers to perform the duties of his office, as determined pursuant to this Section, the duties of his office shall be performed by an acting officer who shall be appointed by the Governor.

(6) DETERMINATION OF INCAPACITY

The General Assembly shall by law prescribe with respect to those officers, other than the Governor, whose offices are created by this Article, procedures for determining the physical or mental incapacity of any officer to perform the duties of his office, and for determining whether an officer who has been temporarily incapacitated has sufficiently recovered his physical or mental capacity to perform the duties of his office. Removal of those officers from office for any other cause shall be by impeachment.

(7) SPECIAL QUALIFICATIONS FOR ATTORNEY GENERAL

Only persons duly authorized to practice law in the courts of this State shall be eligible for appointment or election as Attorney General.

Section 8. Council of State

The Council of State shall consist of the officers whose offices are established by this Article.

Section 9. Compensation and Allowances

The officers whose offices are established by this Article shall at stated periods receive the compensation and allowances prescribed by law, which shall not be diminished during the time for which they have been chosen.

Section 10. Seal of State

There shall be a seal of the State, which shall be kept by the Governor and used by him as occasion may require, and shall be called "The Great Seal of the State of North Carolina". All grants or commissions shall be issued in the name and by the authority of the State of North Carolina, sealed with "The Great Seal of the State of North Carolina", and signed by the Governor.

Section 11. Administrative Departments

Not later than July 1, 1975, all administrative departments, agencies, and offices of the State and their respective functions, powers, and duties shall be allocated by law among and within not more than 25 principal administrative departments so as to group them as far as practicable according to major purposes. Regulatory, quasi-judicial, and temporary agencies may, but need not, be allocated within a principal department.

ARTICLE IV: JUDICIAL

Section 1. Judicial Power

The judicial power of the State shall, except as provided in Section 3 of this Article, be vested in a Court for the Trial of Impeachments and in a General Court of Justice. The General Assembly shall have no power to deprive the judicial department of any power or jurisdiction that rightfully pertains to it as a co-ordinate department of the government, nor shall it establish or authorize any courts other than as permitted by this Article.

Section 2. General Court of Justice

The General Court of Justice shall constitute a unified judicial system for purposes of jurisdiction, operation, and administration, and shall consist of an Appellate Division, a Superior Court Division, and a District Court Division.

Section 3. Judicial Powers of Administrative Agencies

The General Assembly may vest in administrative agencies established pursuant to law such judicial powers as may be reasonably necessary as an incident to the accomplishment of the purposes for which the agencies were created. Appeals from administrative agencies shall be to the General Court of Justice.

Section 4. Court for the Trial of Impeachments

The House of Representatives solely shall have the power of impeaching. The Court for the Trial of Impeachments shall be the Senate. When the Governor or Lieutenant Governor is impeached, the Chief Justice shall preside over the Court. A majority of the members shall be necessary to a quorum, and no person shall be convicted without the concurrence of two-thirds of the Senators present. Judgment upon conviction shall not extend beyond removal from and disqualification to hold office in this State, but the party shall be liable to indictment and punishment according to law.

Section 5. Appellate Division

The Appellate Division of the General Court of Justice shall consist of the Supreme Court and the Court of Appeals.

Section 6. Supreme Court

(1) MEMBERSHIP

The Supreme Court shall consist of a Chief Justice and six Associate Justices, but the General Assembly may increase the number of Associate Justices to not more than eight. In the event the Chief Justice is unable, on account of absence or temporary incapacity, to perform any of the duties placed upon him, the senior Associate Justice available may discharge those duties.

(2) SESSIONS OF THE SUPREME COURT

The sessions of the Supreme Court shall be held in the City of Raleigh unless otherwise provided by the General Assembly.

Section 7. Court of Appeals

The structure, organization, and composition of the Court of Appeals shall be determined by the General Assembly. The Court shall have not less than five members, and may be authorized to sit in divisions, or other than en banc. Sessions of the Court shall be held at such times and places as the General Assembly may prescribe.

Section 8. Retirement of Justices and Judges

The General Assembly shall provide by general law for the retirement of Justices and Judges of the General Court of Justice, and may provide for the temporary recall of any retired Justice or

Judge to serve on the court or courts of the division from which he was retired. The General Assembly shall also prescribe maximum age limits for service as a Justice or Judge.

Section 9. Superior Courts

(1) SUPERIOR COURT DISTRICTS

The General Assembly shall, from time to time, divide the State into a convenient number of Superior Court judicial districts and shall provide for the election of one or more Superior Court Judges for each district. Each regular Superior Court Judge shall reside in the district for which he is elected. The General Assembly may provide by general law for the selection or appointment of special or emergency Superior Court Judges not selected for a particular judicial district.

(2) OPEN AT ALL TIMES; SESSIONS FOR TRIAL OF CASES

The Superior Courts shall be open at all times for the transaction of all business except the trial of issues of fact requiring a jury. Regular trial sessions of the Superior Court shall be held at times fixed pursuant to a calendar of courts promulgated by the Supreme Court. At least two sessions for the trial of jury cases shall be held annually in each county.

(3) CLERKS

A Clerk of the Superior Court for each county shall be elected for a term of four years by the qualified voters thereof, at the same time and places as members of the General Assembly are elected. If the office of Clerk of the Superior Court becomes vacant otherwise than by the expiration of the term, or if the people fail to elect, the senior regular resident Judge of the Superior Court serving the county shall appoint to fill the vacancy until an election can be regularly held.

Section 10. District Courts

The General Assembly shall, from time to time, divide the State into a convenient number of local court districts and shall prescribe where the District Courts shall sit, but a District Court must sit in at least one place in each county. District Judges shall be elected for each district for a term of four years, in a manner prescribed by law. When more than one District Judge is authorized and elected for a district, the Chief Justice of the Supreme Court shall designate one of the judges as Chief District Judge. Every District Judge shall reside in the district for which he is elected. For each county, the senior regular resident Judge of the Superior Court serving the county shall appoint from nominations submitted by the Clerk of the Superior Court of the county, one or more Magistrates who shall be officers of the District Court. The initial term of appointment for a magistrate shall be for two years and subsequent terms shall be for four years. The number of District Judges and Magistrates shall, from time to time, be determined by the General Assembly. Vacancies in the office of District Judge shall be filled for the unexpired term in a manner prescribed by law. Vacancies in the office of Magistrate shall be filled for the unexpired term in the manner provided for original appointment to the office, unless otherwise provided by the General Assembly.

Section 11. Assignment of Judges

The Chief Justice of the Supreme Court, acting in accordance with rules of the Supreme Court, shall make assignments of Judges of the Superior Court and may transfer District Judges from one district to another for temporary or specialized duty. The principle of rotating Superior Court Judges among the various districts of a division is a salutary one and shall be observed. For this purpose the General Assembly may divide the State into a number of judicial divisions. Subject to the general supervision of the Chief Justice of the Supreme Court, assignment of District Judges within each local court district shall be made by the Chief District Judge.

Section 12. Jurisdiction of the General Court of Justice

(1) SUPREME COURT

The Supreme Court shall have jurisdiction to review upon appeal any decision of the courts below, upon any matter of law or legal inference. The jurisdiction of the Supreme Court over "issues of fact" and "questions of fact" shall be the same exercised by it prior to the adoption of this Article, and the Court may issue any remedial writs necessary to give it general supervision and control over the proceedings of the other courts. The Supreme Court also has jurisdiction to review, when authorized by law, direct appeals from a final order or decision of the North Carolina Utilities Commission.

(2) COURT OF APPEALS

The Court of Appeals shall have such appellate jurisdiction as the General Assembly may prescribe.

(3) SUPERIOR COURT

Except as otherwise provided by the General Assembly, the Superior Court shall have original general jurisdiction throughout the State. The Clerks of the Superior Court shall have such jurisdiction and powers as the General Assembly shall prescribe by general law uniformly applicable in every county of the State.

(4) DISTRICT COURTS; MAGISTRATES

The General Assembly shall, by general law uniformly applicable in every local court district of the State, prescribe the jurisdiction and powers of the District Courts and Magistrates.

(5) WAIVER

The General Assembly may by general law provide that the jurisdictional limits may be waived in civil cases.

(6) APPEALS

The General Assembly shall by general law provide a proper system of appeals. Appeals from Magistrates shall be heard de novo, with the right of trial by jury as defined in this Constitution and the laws of this State.

Section 13. Forms of action; rules of procedure

(1) FORMS OF ACTION

There shall be in this State but one form of action for the enforcement or protection of private rights or the redress of private wrongs, which shall be denominated a civil action, and in which there shall be a right to have issues of fact tried before a jury. Every action prosecuted by the people of the State as a party against a person charged with a public offense, for the punishment thereof, shall be termed a criminal action.

(2) RULES OF PROCEDURE

The Supreme Court shall have exclusive authority to make rules of procedure and practice for the Appellate Division. The General Assembly may make rules of procedure and practice for the Superior Court and District Court Divisions, and the General Assembly may delegate this authority to the Supreme Court. No rule of procedure or practice shall abridge substantive rights or abrogate or limit the right of trial by jury. If the General Assembly should delegate to the Supreme Court the rule-making power, the General Assembly may, nevertheless, alter, amend, or repeal any rule of procedure or practice adopted by the Supreme Court for the Superior Court or District Court Divisions.

Section 14. Waiver of Jury Trial

In all issues of fact joined in any court, the parties in any civil case may waive the right to have the issues determined by a jury, in which case the finding of the judge upon the facts shall have the force and effect of a verdict by a jury.

Section 15. Administration

The General Assembly shall provide for an administrative office of the courts to carry out the provisions of this Article.

Section 16. Terms of Office and Election of Justices of the Supreme Court, Judges of the Court of Appeals, and Judges of the Superior Court

Justices of the Supreme Court, Judges of the Court of Appeals, and regular Judges of the Superior Court shall be elected by the qualified voters and shall hold office for terms of eight years and until their successors are elected and qualified. Justices of the Supreme Court and Judges of the Court of Appeals shall be elected by the qualified voters of the State. Regular Judges of the Superior Court may be elected by the qualified voters of the State or by the voters of their respective districts, as the General Assembly may prescribe.

Section 17. Removal of Judges, Magistrates and Clerks

(1) REMOVAL OF JUDGES BY THE GENERAL ASSEMBLY

Any Justice or Judge of the General Court of Justice may be removed from office for mental or physical incapacity by joint resolution of two-thirds of all the members of each house of the General Assembly. Any Justice or Judge against whom the General Assembly may be about to proceed shall receive notice thereof, accompanied by a copy of the causes alleged for his removal, at least 20 days before the day on which either house of the General Assembly shall act thereon. Removal from office by the General Assembly for any other cause shall be by impeachment.

(2) ADDITIONAL METHOD OF REMOVAL OF JUDGES

The General Assembly shall prescribe a procedure, in addition to impeachment and address set forth in this Section, for the removal of a Justice or Judge of the General Court of Justice for mental or physical incapacity interfering with the performance of his duties which is, or is likely to become, permanent, and for the censure and removal of a Justice or Judge of the General Court of Justice for wilful misconduct in office, wilful and persistent failure to perform his duties, habitual intemperance, conviction of a crime involving moral turpitude, or conduct prejudicial to the administration of justice that brings the judicial office into disrepute.

(3) REMOVAL OF MAGISTRATES

The General Assembly shall provide by general law for the removal of Magistrates for misconduct or mental or physical incapacity.

(4) REMOVAL OF CLERKS

Any Clerk of the Superior Court may be removed from office for misconduct or mental or physical incapacity by the senior regular resident Superior Court Judge serving the county. Any Clerk against whom proceedings are instituted shall receive written notice of the charges against him at least 10 days before the hearing upon the charges. Any Clerk so removed from office shall be entitled to an appeal as provided by law.

Section 18. District Attorney and Prosecutorial Districts

(1) DISTRICT ATTORNEYS

The General Assembly shall, from time to time, divide the State into a convenient number of prosecutorial districts, for each of which a District Attorney shall be chosen for a term of four years by the qualified voters thereof, at the same time and places as members of the General Assembly are elected. Only persons duly authorized to practice law in the courts of this State shall be eligible for election or appointment as a District Attorney. The District Attorney shall advise the officers of justice in his district, be responsible for the prosecution on behalf of the State of all criminal actions in the Superior Courts of his district, perform such duties related to appeals therefrom as the Attorney General may require, and perform such other duties as the General Assembly may prescribe.

(2) PROSECUTION IN DISTRICT COURT DIVISION

Criminal actions in the District Court Division shall be prosecuted in such manner as the General Assembly may prescribe by general law uniformly applicable in every local court district of the State.

Section 19. Vacancies

Unless otherwise provided in this Article, all vacancies occurring in the offices provided for by this Article shall be filled by appointment of the Governor, and the appointees shall hold their places until the next election for members of the General Assembly that is held more than 60 days after the vacancy occurs, when elections shall be held to fill the offices. When the unexpired term of any of the offices named in this Article of the Constitution in which a vacancy has occurred, and in which it is herein provided that the Governor shall fill the vacancy, expires on the first day of January succeeding the next election for members of the General Assembly, the Governor shall appoint to fill that vacancy for the unexpired term of the office. If any person elected or appointed to any of these offices shall fail to qualify, the office shall be appointed to, held and filled as provided in case of vacancies occurring therein. All incumbents of these offices shall hold until their successors are qualified.

Section 20. Revenues and Expenses of the Judicial Department

The General Assembly shall provide for the establishment of a schedule of court fees and costs which shall be uniform throughout the State within each division of the General Court of Justice. The operating expenses of the judicial department, other than compensation to process servers and other locally paid non-judicial officers, shall be paid from State funds.

Section 21. Fees, Salaries, and Emoluments

The General Assembly shall prescribe and regulate the fees, salaries, and emoluments of all officers provided for in this Article, but the salaries of Judges shall not be diminished during their continuance in office. In no case shall the compensation of any Judge or Magistrate be dependent upon his decision or upon the collection of costs.

Section 22. Qualification of Justices and Judges

Only persons duly authorized to practice law in the courts of this State shall be eligible for election or appointment as a Justice of the Supreme Court, Judge of the Court of Appeals, Judge of the Superior Court, or Judge of District Court. This section shall not apply to persons elected to or serving in such capacities on or before January 1, 1981.

ARTICLE V: FINANCE

Section 1. No Capitation Tax to be Levied

No poll or capitation tax shall be levied by the General Assembly or by any county, city or town, or other taxing unit.

Section 2. State and Local Taxation

(1) POWER OF TAXATION

The power of taxation shall be exercised in a just and equitable manner, for public purposes only, and shall never be surrendered, suspended, or contracted away.

(2) CLASSIFICATION

Only the General Assembly shall have the power to classify property for taxation, which power shall be exercised only on a State-wide basis and shall not be delegated. No class of property shall be taxed except by uniform rule, and every classification shall be made by general law uniformly applicable in every county, city and town, and other unit of local government.

(3) EXEMPTIONS

Property belonging to the State, counties, and municipal corporations shall be exempt from taxation. The General Assembly may exempt cemeteries and property held for educational, scientific, literary, cultural, charitable, or religious purposes, and, to a value not exceeding $300, any personal property. The General Assembly may exempt from taxation not exceeding $1,000 in value of property held and used as the place of residence of the owner. Every exemption shall be on a State-wide basis and shall be made by general law uniformly applicable in every county, city and town, and other unit of local government. No taxing authority other than the General Assembly may grant exemptions, and the General Assembly shall not delegate the powers accorded to it by this subsection.

(4) SPECIAL TAX AREAS

Subject to the limitations imposed by Section 4, the General Assembly may enact general laws authorizing the governing body of any county, city, or town to define territorial areas and to levy taxes within those areas, in addition to those levied throughout the county, city, or town, in order to finance, provide, or maintain services, facilities, and functions in addition to or to a greater extent than those financed, provided, or maintained for the entire county, city, or town.

(5) PURPOSES OF PROPERTY TAX

The General Assembly shall not authorize any county, city or town, special district, or other unit of local government to levy taxes on property, except for purposes authorized by general law uniformly applicable throughout the State, unless the tax is approved by a majority of the qualified voters of the unit who vote thereon.

(6) INCOME TAX

The rate of tax on incomes shall not in any case exceed ten percent, and there shall be allowed personal exemptions and deductions so that only net incomes are taxed.

(7) CONTRACTS

The General Assembly may enact laws whereby the State, any county, city or town, and any other public corporation may contract with and appropriate money to any person, association, or corporation for the accomplishment of public purposes only.

Section 3. Limitations Upon The Increase of State Debt

(1) AUTHORIZED PURPOSES; TWO-THIRDS LIMITATION

The General Assembly shall have no power to contract debts secured by a pledge of the faith and credit of the State, unless approved by a majority of the qualified voters of the State who vote thereon, except for the following purposes:

(a) to fund or refund a valid existing debt;

(b) to supply an unforeseen deficiency in the revenue;

(c) to borrow in anticipation of the collection of taxes due and payable within the current fiscal year to an amount not exceeding 50 per cent of such taxes;

(d) to suppress riots or insurrections, or to repel invasions;

(e) to meet emergencies immediately threatening the public health or safety, as conclusively determined in writing by the Governor;

(f) for any other lawful purpose, to the extent of two-thirds of the amount by which the State's outstanding indebtedness shall have been reduced during the next preceding biennium.

(2) GIFT OR LOAN OF CREDIT REGULATED

The General Assembly shall have no power to give or lend the credit of the State in aid of any person, association, or corporation, except a corporation in which the State has a controlling interest, unless the subject is submitted to a direct vote of the people of the State, and is approved by a majority of the qualified voters who vote thereon.

(3) DEFINITIONS

A debt is incurred within the meaning of this Section when the State borrows money. A pledge of the faith and credit within the meaning of this Section is a pledge of the taxing power. A loan of credit within the meaning of this Section occurs when the State exchanges its obligations with or in any way guarantees the debts of an individual, association, or private corporation.

(4) CERTAIN DEBTS BARRED

The General Assembly shall never assume or pay any debt or obligation, express or implied, incurred in aid of insurrection or rebellion against the United States. Neither shall the General Assembly assume or pay any debt or bond incurred or issued by authority of the Convention of 1868, the special session of the General Assembly of 1868, or the General Assemblies of 1868-69 and 1869-70, unless the subject is submitted to the people of the State and is approved by a majority of all the qualified voters at a referendum held for that sole purpose.

(5) OUTSTANDING DEBT

Except as provided in subsection (4), nothing in this Section shall be construed to invalidate or impair the obligation of any bond, note, or other evidence of indebtedness outstanding or authorized for issue as of July 1, 1973.

Section 4. Limitations Upon the Increase of Local Government Debt

(1) REGULATION OF BORROWING AND DEBT

The General Assembly shall enact general laws relating to the borrowing of money secured by a pledge of the faith and credit and the contracting of other debts by counties, cities and towns, special districts, and other units, authorities, and agencies of local government.

(2) AUTHORIZED PURPOSES; TWO-THIRDS LIMITATION

The General Assembly shall have no power to authorize any county, city or town, special district, or other unit of local government to contract debts secured by a pledge of its faith and credit unless approved by a majority of the qualified voters of the unit who vote thereon, except for the following purposes:

(a) to fund or refund a valid existing debt;

(b) to supply an unforeseen deficiency in the revenue;

(c) to borrow in anticipation of the collection of taxes due and payable within the current fiscal year to an amount not exceeding 50 per cent of such taxes;

(d) to suppress riots or insurrections;

(e) to meet emergencies immediately threatening the public health or safety, as conclusively determined in writing by the Governor;

(f) for purposes authorized by general laws uniformly applicable throughout the State, to the extent of two-thirds of the amount by which the unit's outstanding indebtedness shall have been reduced during the next preceding fiscal year.

(3) GIFT OR LOAN OF CREDIT REGULATED

No county, city or town, special district, or other unit of local government shall give or lend its credit in aid of any person, association, or corporation, except for public purposes as authorized by general law, and unless approved by a majority of the qualified voters of the unit who vote thereon.

(4) CERTAIN DEBTS BARRED

No county, city or town, or other unit of local government shall assume or pay any debt or the interest thereon contracted directly or indirectly in aid or support of rebellion or insurrection against the United States.

(5) DEFINITIONS

A debt is incurred within the meaning of this Section when a county, city or town, special district, or other unit, authority, or agency of local government borrows money. A pledge of faith and credit within the meaning of this Section is a pledge of the taxing power. A loan of credit within the meaning of this Section occurs when a county, city or town, special district, or other unit, authority, or agency of local government exchanges its obligations with or in any way guarantees the debts of an individual, association, or private corporation.

(6) OUTSTANDING DEBT

Except as provided in subsection (4), nothing in this Section shall be construed to invalidate or impair the obligation of any bond, note, or other evidence of indebtedness outstanding or authorized for issue as of July 1, 1973.

Section 5. Acts Levying Taxes to State Objects

Every act of the General Assembly levying a tax shall state the special object to which it is to be applied, and it shall be applied to no other purpose.

Section 6. Inviolability of Sinking Funds and Retirement Funds

(1) Sinking Funds

The General Assembly shall not use or authorize to be used any part of the amount of any sinking fund for any purpose other than the retirement of the bonds for which the sinking fund has been created, except that these funds may be invested as authorized by law.

(2) RETIREMENT FUNDS

Neither the General Assembly nor any public officer, employee, or agency shall use or authorize to be used any part of the funds of the Teachers' and State Employees' Retirement System or the Local Governmental Employees' Retirement System for any purpose other than retirement system benefits and purposes, administrative expenses, and refunds; except that retirement system funds may be invested as authorized by law, subject to the investment limitation that the funds of the Teachers' and State Employees' Retirement System and the Local Governmental Employees' Retirement System shall not be applied, diverted, loaned to, or used by the State, any State agency, State officer, public officer, or public employee.

Section 7. Drawing Public Money

(1) STATE TREASURY

No money shall be drawn from the State treasury but in consequence of appropriations made by law, and an accurate account of the receipts and expenditures of State funds shall be published annually.

(2) LOCAL TREASURY

No money shall be drawn from the treasury of any county, city or town, or other unit of local government except by authority of law.

Section 8. Health Care Facilities

Notwithstanding any other provisions of this Constitution, the General Assembly may enact general laws to authorize the State, counties, cities or towns, and other State and local governmental entities to issue revenue bonds to finance or refinance for any such governmental entity or any nonprofit private corporation, regardless of any church or religious relationship, the cost of acquiring, constructing, and financing health care facility projects to be operated to serve and benefit the public; provided, no cost incurred earlier than two years prior to the effective date of this section shall be refinanced. Such bonds shall be payable from the revenues, gross or net, of any such projects and any other health care facilities of any such governmental entity or nonprofit private corporation pledged therefor; shall not be secured by a pledge of the full faith and credit, or deemed to create an indebtedness requiring voter approval of any governmental entity; and may be secured by an agreement which may provide for the conveyance of title of, with or without consideration, any such project or facilities to the governmental entity or nonprofit private corporation. The power of eminent domain shall not be used pursuant hereto for nonprofit private corporations.

Section 9. Capital Projects for Industry

Notwithstanding any other provision of this Constitution, the General Assembly may enact general laws to authorize counties to create authorities to issue revenue bonds to finance, but not to refinance, the cost of capital projects consisting of industrial, manufacturing and pollution control facilities for industry and pollution control facilities for public utilities, and to refund such bonds.

In no event shall such revenue bonds be secured by or payable from any public moneys whatsoever, but such revenue bonds shall be secured by and payable only from revenues or property derived from private parties. All such capital projects and all transactions therefor shall be subject to taxation to the extent

such projects and transactions would be subject to taxation if no public body were involved therewith; provided, however, that the General Assembly may provide that the interest on such revenue bonds shall be exempt from income taxes within the State.
The power of eminent domain shall not be exercised to provide any property for any such capital project.

Section 10. Joint Ownership of Generation and Transmission Facilities

In addition to other powers conferred upon them by law, municipalities owning or operating facilities for the generation, transmission or distribution of electric power and energy and joint agencies formed by such municipalities for the purpose of owning or operating facilities for the generation and transmission of electric power and energy (each, respectively, "a unit of municipal government") may jointly or severally own, operate and maintain works, plants and facilities, within or without the State, for the generation and transmission of electric power and energy, or both, with any person, firm, association or corporation, public or private, engaged in the generation, transmission or distribution of electric power and energy for resale (each, respectively, "a co-owner") within this State or any state contiguous to this State, and may enter into and carry out agreements with respect to such jointly owned facilities. For the purpose of financing its share of the cost of any such jointly owned electric generation or transmission facilities, a unit of municipal government may issue its revenue bonds in the manner prescribed by the General Assembly, payable as to both principal and interest solely from and secured by a lien and charge on all or any part of the revenue derived, or to be derived, by such unit of municipal government from the ownership and operation of its electric facilities; provided, however, that no unit of municipal government shall be liable, either jointly or severally, for any acts, omissions or obligations of any co-owner, nor shall any money or property of any unit of municipal government be credited or otherwise applied to the account of any co-owner or be charged with any debt, lien or mortgage as a result of any debt or obligation of any co-owner.

Section 11. Capital Projects for Agriculture

Notwithstanding any other provision of the Constitution the General Assembly may enact general laws to authorize the creation of an agency to issue revenue bonds to finance the cost of capital projects consisting of agricultural facilities, and to refund such bonds.

In no event shall such revenue bonds be secured by or payable from any public moneys whatsoever, but such revenue bonds shall be secured by and payable only from revenues or property derived from private parties. All such capital projects and all transactions therefor shall be subject to taxation to the extent such projects and transactions would be subject to taxation if no public body were involved therewith; provided, however, that the General Assembly may provide that the interest on such revenue bonds shall be exempt from income taxes within the State. The power of eminent domain shall not be exercised to provide any property for any such capital project.

Section 12. Higher Education Facilities

Notwithstanding any other provisions of this Constitution, the General Assembly may enact general laws to authorize the State or any State entity to issue revenue bonds to finance and refinance the cost of acquiring, constructing, and financing higher education facilities to be operated to serve and benefit the public for any nonprofit private corporation, regardless of any church or religious relationship provided no cost incurred earlier than five years prior to the effective date of this section shall be refinanced. Such bonds shall be payable from any revenues or assets of any such nonprofit private corporation pledged therefor, shall not be secured by a pledge of the full faith and credit of the State or such State entity or deemed to create an indebtedness requiring voter approval of the State or such entity, and, where the title to such facilities is vested in the State or any State entity, may be secured by an agreement which may provide for the conveyance of title to, with or without consideration, such facilities to the nonprofit private corporation. The power of eminent domain shall not be used pursuant hereto.

Section 13. Seaport and Airport Facilities

(1) Notwithstanding any other provision of this Constitution, the General Assembly may enact general laws to grant to the State, counties, municipalities, and other State and local governmental entities all powers useful in connection with the development of new and existing seaports and airports, and to authorize such public bodies:

(a) to acquire, construct, own, own jointly with public and private parties, lease as lessee, mortgage, sell, lease as lessor, or otherwise dispose of lands and facilities and improvements, including undivided interest therein;

(b) to finance and refinance for public and private parties seaport and airport facilities and improvements which relate to, develop or further waterborne or airborne commerce and cargo and passenger traffic, including commercial, industrial, manufacturing, processing, mining, transportation, distribution, storage, marine, aviation and environmental facilities and improvements; and

(c) to secure any such financing or refinancing by all or any portion of their revenues, income or assets or other available monies associated with any of their seaport or airport facilities and with the facilities and improvements to be financed or refinanced, and by foreclosable liens on all or any part of their properties associated with any of their seaport or airport facilities and with the facilities and improvements to be financed or refinanced, but in no event to create a debt secured by a pledge of the faith and credit of the State or any other public body in the State.

Section 14. Project Development Financing

Notwithstanding Section 4 of this Article, the General Assembly may enact general laws authorizing any county, city, or town to define territorial areas in the county, city, or town and borrow money to be used to finance public improvements associated with private development projects within the territorial areas, as provided in this section. The General Assembly shall set forth by statute the method for determining the size of the territorial area and the issuing unit. This method is conclusive. When a territorial area is defined pursuant to this section, the county shall determine the current assessed value of taxable real and personal property in the territorial area. Thereafter, property in the territorial area continues to be subject to taxation to the same extent and in like manner as property not in the territorial area, but the net proceeds of taxes levied on the excess, if any, of the assessed value of taxable real and personal property in the territorial area at the time the taxes are levied over the assessed value of taxable real and personal property in the territorial area at the time the territorial area was defined may be set aside. The instruments of indebtedness authorized by this section shall be secured by these set-aside proceeds. The General Assembly may authorize a county, city, or town issuing these instruments of indebtedness to pledge, as additional security, revenues available to the issuing unit from sources other than the issuing unit's exercise of its taxing power. As long as no revenues are pledged other than the set-aside proceeds authorized by this section and the revenues authorized in the preceding sentence, these instruments of indebtedness may be issued without approval by referendum. The county, city, or town may not pledge as security for these instruments of indebtedness any property tax revenues other than the set-aside proceeds authorized in this section, or in any other manner pledge its full faith and credit as security for these instruments of indebtedness unless a vote of the people is held as required by and in compliance with the requirements of Section 4 of this Article.

Notwithstanding the provisions of Section 2 of this Article, the General Assembly may enact general laws authorizing a county, city, or town that has defined a territorial area pursuant to this section to assess property within the territorial area at a minimum value if agreed to by the owner of the property, which agreed minimum value shall be binding on the current owner and any future owners as long as the defined territorial area is in effect.

ARTICLE VI: SUFFRAGE AND ELIGIBILITY TO OFFICE

Section 1. Who May Vote

Every person born in the United States and every person who has been naturalized, 18 years of age, and possessing the qualifications set out in this Article, shall be entitled to vote at any election by the people of the State, except as herein otherwise provided.

Section 2. Qualifications of Voter

(1) RESIDENCE PERIOD FOR STATE ELECTIONS

Any person who has resided in the State of North Carolina for one year and in the precinct, ward, or other election district for 30 days next preceding an election, and possesses the other qualifications set out in this Article, shall be entitled to vote at any election held in this State. Removal from one precinct, ward, or other election district to another in this State shall not operate to deprive any person of the right to vote in the precinct, ward, or other election district from which that person has removed until 30 days after the removal.

(2) RESIDENCE PERIOD FOR PRESIDENTIAL ELECTIONS

The General Assembly may reduce the time of residence for persons voting in presidential elections. A person made eligible by reason of a reduction in time of residence shall possess the other qualifications set out in this Article, shall only be entitled to vote for President and Vice President of the United States or for electors for President and Vice President, and shall not thereby become eligible to hold office in this State.

(3) DISQUALIFICATION OF FELON

No person adjudged guilty of a felony against this State or the United States, or adjudged guilty of a felony in another state that also would be a felony if it had been committed in this State, shall be permitted to vote unless that person shall be first restored to the rights of citizenship in the manner prescribed by law.

Section 3. Registration

Every person offering to vote shall be at the time legally registered as a voter as herein prescribed and in the manner provided by law. The General Assembly shall enact general laws governing the registration of voters.

Section 4. Qualification for Registration

Every person presenting himself for registration shall be able to read and write any section of the Constitution in the English language.

Section 5. Elections by People and General Assembly

All elections by the people shall be by ballot, and all elections by the General Assembly shall be viva voce. A contested election for any office established by Article III of this Constitution shall be determined by joint ballot of both houses of the General Assembly in the manner prescribed by law.

Section 6. Eligibility to Elective Office

Every qualified voter in North Carolina who is 21 years of age, except as in this Constitution disqualified, shall be eligible for election by the people to office.

Section 7. Oath

Before entering upon the duties of an office, a person elected or appointed to the office shall take and subscribe the following oath:

"I, _____, do solemnly swear (or affirm) that I will support and maintain the Constitution and laws of the United States, and the Constitution and laws of North Carolina not inconsistent therewith, and that I will faithfully discharge the duties of my office as _____, so help me God."

Section 8. Disqualifications for Office

The following persons shall be disqualified for office:
First, any person who shall deny the being of Almighty God.
Second, with respect to any office that is filled by election by the people, any person who is not qualified to vote in an election for that office.

Third, any person who has been adjudged guilty of treason or any other felony against this State or the United States, or any person who has been adjudged guilty of a felony in another state that also would be a felony if it had been committed in this State, or any person who has been adjudged guilty of corruption or malpractice in any office, or any person who has been removed by impeachment from any office, and who has not been restored to the rights of citizenship in the manner prescribed by law.

Section 9. Dual Office Holding

(1) PROHIBITIONS

It is salutary that the responsibilities of self-government be widely shared among the citizens of the State and that the potential abuse of authority inherent in the holding of multiple offices by an individual be avoided. Therefore, no person who holds any office or place of trust or profit under the United States or any department thereof, or under any other state or government, shall be eligible to hold any office in this State that is filled by election by the people. No person shall hold concurrently any two offices in this State that are filled by election of the people. No person shall hold concurrently any two or more appointive offices or places of trust or profit, or any combination of elective and appointive offices or places of trust or profit, except as the General Assembly shall provide by general law.

(2) EXCEPTIONS

The provisions of this Section shall not prohibit any officer of the military forces of the State or of the United States not on active duty for an extensive period of time, any notary public, or any delegate to a Convention of the People from holding concurrently another office or place of trust or profit under this State or the United States or any department thereof.

Section 10. Continuation in Office

In the absence of any contrary provision, all officers in this State, whether appointed or elected, shall hold their positions until other appointments are made or, if the offices are elective, until their successors are chosen and qualified.

ARTICLE VII: LOCAL GOVERNMENT

Section 1. General Assembly to Provide for Local Government

The General Assembly shall provide for the organization and government and the fixing of boundaries of counties, cities and towns, and other governmental subdivisions, and, except as otherwise prohibited by this Constitution, may give such powers and duties to counties, cities and towns, and other governmental subdivisions as it may deem advisable.

The General Assembly shall not incorporate as a city or town, nor shall it authorize to be incorporated as a city or town, any territory lying within one mile of the corporate limits of any other city or town having a population of 5,000 or more according to the most recent decennial census of population taken by order of Congress, or lying within three miles of the corporate limits of any other city or town having a population of 10,000 or more according to the most recent decennial census of population taken by order of Congress, or lying within four miles of the corporate limits of any other city or town having a population of 25,000 or more according to the most recent decennial census of population taken by order of Congress, or lying within five miles of the corporate limits of any other city or town having a population of 50,000 or more according to the most recent decennial census of population taken by order of Congress. Notwithstanding the foregoing limitations, the General Assembly may incorporate a city or town by an act adopted by vote of three-fifths of all the members of each house.

Section 2. Sheriffs

In each county a Sheriff shall be elected by the qualified voters thereof at the same time and places as members of the General Assembly are elected and shall hold his office for a period of four years, subject to removal for cause as provided by law. No person is eligible to serve as Sheriff if that person has been convicted of a felony against this State, the United States, or another state, whether or not that person has been restored to the rights of citizenship in the manner prescribed by law. Convicted of a felony includes the entry of a plea of guilty; a verdict or finding of guilt by a jury, judge, magistrate, or other adjudicating body, tribunal, or official, either civilian or military; or a plea of no contest, nolo contendere, or the equivalent.

Section 3. Merged or Consolidated Counties

Any unit of local government formed by the merger or consolidation of a county or counties and the cities and towns therein shall be deemed both a county and a city for the purposes of this Constitution, and may exercise any authority conferred by law on counties, or on cities and towns, or both, as the General Assembly may provide.

ARTICLE VIII: CORPORATIONS

Section 1. Corporate Charters

No corporation shall be created, nor shall its charter be extended, altered, or amended by special act, except corporations for charitable, educational, penal, or reformatory purposes that are to be and remain under the patronage and control of the State; but the General Assembly shall provide by general laws for the chartering, organization, and powers of all corporations, and for the amending, extending, and forfeiture of all charters, except those above permitted by special act. All such general acts may be altered from time to time or repealed. The General Assembly may at any time by special act repeal the charter of any corporation.

Section 2. Corporations Defined

The term "corporation" as used in this Section shall be construed to include all associations and joint-stock companies having any of the powers and privileges of corporations not possessed by individuals or partnerships. All corporations shall have the right to sue and shall be subject to be sued in all courts, in like cases as natural persons.

ARTICLE IX: EDUCATION

Section 1. Education Encouraged

Religion, morality, and knowledge being necessary to good government and the happiness of mankind, schools, libraries, and the means of education shall forever be encouraged.

Section 2. Uniform System of Schools

(1) GENERAL AND UNIFORM SYSTEM: TERM

The General Assembly shall provide by taxation and otherwise for a general and uniform system of free public schools, which shall be maintained at least nine months in every year, and wherein equal opportunities shall be provided for all students.

(2) LOCAL RESPONSIBILITY

The General Assembly may assign to units of local government such responsibility for the financial support of the free public schools as it may deem appropriate. The governing boards of units of local government with financial responsibility for public education may use local revenues to add to or supplement any public school or post-secondary school program.

Section 3. School Attendance

The General Assembly shall provide that every child of appropriate age and of sufficient mental and physical ability shall attend the public schools, unless educated by other means.

Section 4. State Board of Education

(1) BOARD

The State Board of Education shall consist of the Lieutenant Governor, the Treasurer, and eleven members appointed by the

Governor, subject to confirmation by the General Assembly in joint session. The General Assembly shall divide the State into eight educational districts. Of the appointive members of the Board, one shall be appointed from each of the eight educational districts and three shall be appointed from the State at large. Appointments shall be for overlapping terms of eight years. Appointments to fill vacancies shall be made by the Governor for the unexpired terms and shall not be subject to confirmation.

(2) SUPERINTENDENT OF PUBLIC INSTRUCTION

The Superintendent of Public Instruction shall be the secretary and chief administrative officer of the State Board of Education.

Section 5. Powers and Duties of Board

The State Board of Education shall supervise and administer the free public school system and the educational funds provided for its support, except the funds mentioned in Section 7 of this Article, and shall make all needed rules and regulations in relation thereto, subject to laws enacted by the General Assembly.

Section 6. State School Fund

The proceeds of all lands that have been or hereafter may be granted by the United States to this State, and not otherwise appropriated by this State or the United States; all moneys, stocks, bonds, and other property belonging to the State for purposes of public education; the net proceeds of all sales of the swamp lands belonging to the State; and all other grants, gifts, and devises that have been or hereafter may be made to the State, and not otherwise appropriated by the State or by the terms of the grant, gift, or devise, shall be paid into the State Treasury and, together with so much of the revenue of the State as may be set apart for that purpose, shall be faithfully appropriated and used exclusively for establishing and maintaining a uniform system of free public schools.

Section 7. County School Fund; State Fund for Certain Moneys

(a) Except as provided in subsection (b) of this section, all moneys, stocks, bonds, and other property belonging to a county school fund, and the clear proceeds of all penalties and forfeitures and of all fines collected in the several counties for any breach of the penal laws of the State, shall belong to and remain in the several counties, and shall be faithfully appropriated and used exclusively for maintaining free public schools.

(b) The General Assembly may place in a State fund the clear proceeds of all civil penalties, forfeitures, and fines which are collected by State agencies and which belong to the public schools pursuant to subsection **(a)** of this section. Moneys in such State fund shall be faithfully appropriated by the General Assembly, on a per pupil basis, to the counties, to be used exclusively for maintaining free public schools.

Section 8. Higher Education

The General Assembly shall maintain a public system of higher education, comprising The University of North Carolina and such other institutions of higher education as the General Assembly may deem wise. The General Assembly shall provide for the selection of trustees of The University of North Carolina and of the other institutions of higher education, in whom shall be vested all the privileges, rights, franchises, and endowments heretofore granted to or conferred upon the trustees of these institutions. The General Assembly may enact laws necessary and expedient for the maintenance and management of The University of North Carolina and the other public institutions of higher education.

Section 9. Benefits of Public Institutions of Higher Education

The General Assembly shall provide that the benefits of The University of North Carolina and other public institutions of higher education, as far as practicable, be extended to the people of the State free of expense.

Section 10. Escheats

(1) ESCHEATS PRIOR TO JULY 1, 1971

All property that prior to July 1, 1971, accrued to the State from escheats, unclaimed dividends, or distributive shares of the estates of deceased persons shall be appropriated to the use of The University of North Carolina.

(2) ESCHEATS AFTER JUNE 30, 1971

All property that, after June 30, 1971, shall accrue to the State from escheats, unclaimed dividends, or distributive shares of the estates of deceased persons shall be used to aid worthy and needy students who are residents of this State and are enrolled in public institutions of higher education in this State. The method, amount, and type of distribution shall be prescribed by law.

ARTICLE X: HOMESTEADS AND EXEMPTIONS

Section 1. Personal Property Exemptions

The personal property of any resident of this State, to a value fixed by the General Assembly but not less than $500, to be selected by the resident, is exempted from sale under execution or other final process of any court, issued for the collection of any debt.

Section 2. Homestead Exemptions

(1) EXEMPTION FROM SALE; EXCEPTIONS

Every homestead and the dwellings and buildings used therewith, to a value fixed by the General Assembly but not less than $1,000, to be selected by the owner thereof, or in lieu thereof, at the option of the owner, any lot in a city or town with the dwellings and buildings used thereon, and to the same value, owned and occupied by a resident of the State, shall be exempt from sale under execution or other final process obtained on any debt. But no property shall be exempt from sale for taxes, or for payment of obligations contracted for its purchase.

(2) EXEMPTION FOR BENEFIT OF CHILDREN

The homestead, after the death of the owner thereof, shall be exempt from the payment of any debt during the minority of the owner's children, or any of them.

(3) EXEMPTION FOR BENEFIT OF SURVIVING SPOUSE

If the owner of a homestead dies, leaving a surviving spouse but no minor children, the homestead shall be exempt from the debts of the owner, and the rents and profits thereof shall inure to the benefit of the surviving spouse until he or she remarries, unless the surviving spouse is the owner of a separate homestead.

(4) CONVEYANCE OF HOMESTEAD

Nothing contained in this Article shall operate to prevent the owner of a homestead from disposing of it by deed, but no deed made by a married owner of a homestead shall be valid without the signature and acknowledgment of his or her spouse.

Section 3. Mechanics And Laborers Liens

The General Assembly shall provide by proper legislation for giving to mechanics and laborers an adequate lien on the subject-matter of their labor. The provisions of Sections 1 and 2 of this Article shall not be so construed as to prevent a laborer's lien for work done and performed for the person claiming the exemption or a mechanic's lien for work done on the premises.

Section 4. Property of Married Women Secured to Them

The real and personal property of any female in this State acquired before marriage, and all property, real and personal, to which she may, after marriage, become in any manner entitled, shall be and remain the sole and separate estate and property of such female, and shall not be liable for any debts, obligations, or engagements of her husband, and may be devised and bequeathed and conveyed by her, subject to such regulations and limitations as the General Assembly may prescribe. Every married woman may exercise powers of attorney conferred upon her by her husband, including the power to execute and acknowledge deeds to property owned by herself and her husband or by her husband.

Section 5. Insurance

A person may insure his or her own life for the sole use and benefit of his or her spouse or children or both, and upon his or her death the proceeds from the insurance shall be paid to or for the benefit of the spouse or children or both, or to a guardian, free from all claims of the representatives or creditors of the insured or his or her estate. Any insurance policy which insures the life of a person for the sole use and benefit of that person's spouse or children or both shall not be subject to the claims of creditors of the insured during his or her lifetime, whether or not the policy reserves to the insured during his or her lifetime any or all rights provided for by the policy and whether or not the policy proceeds are payable to the estate of the insured in the event the beneficiary or beneficiaries predecease the insured.

ARTICLE XI: PUNISHMENTS, CORRECTIONS, AND CHARITIES

Section 1. Punishments

The following punishments only shall be known to the laws of this State: death, imprisonment, fines, suspension of a jail or prison term with or without conditions, restitution, community service, restraints on liberty, work programs, removal from office, and disqualification to hold and enjoy any office of honor, trust, or profit under this State.

Section 2. Death Punishment

The object of punishments being not only to satisfy justice, but also to reform the offender and thus prevent crime, murder, arson, burglary, and rape, and these only, may be punishable with death, if the General Assembly shall so enact.

Section 3. Charitable and Correctional Institutions and Agencies

Such charitable, benevolent, penal, and correctional institutions and agencies as the needs of humanity and the public good may require shall be established and operated by the State under such organization and in such manner as the General Assembly may prescribe.

Section 4. Welfare Policy; Board of Public Welfare

Beneficent provision for the poor, the unfortunate, and the orphan is one of the first duties of a civilized and a Christian state. Therefore the General Assembly shall provide for and define the duties of a board of public welfare.

ARTICLE XII: MILITARY FORCES

Section 1. Governor is Commander in Chief

The Governor shall be Commander in Chief of the military forces of the State and may call out those forces to execute the law, suppress riots and insurrections, and repel invasion.

ARTICLE XIII: CONVENTIONS; CONSTITUTIONAL AMENDMENT AND REVISION

Section 1. Convention of the People

No Convention of the People of this State shall ever be called unless by the concurrence of two-thirds of all the members of each house of the General Assembly, and unless the proposition "Convention or No Convention" is first submitted to the qualified voters of the State at the time and in the manner prescribed by the General Assembly. If a majority of the votes cast upon the proposition are in favor of a Convention, it shall assemble on the day prescribed by the General Assembly. The General Assembly shall, in the act submitting the convention proposition, propose limitations upon the authority of the Convention; and if a majority of the votes cast upon the proposition are in favor of a Convention, those limitations shall become binding upon the Convention. Delegates to the Convention shall be elected by the qualified voters at the time and in the manner prescribed in the act of submission. The Convention shall consist of a number of delegates equal to the membership of the House of Representatives of the General Assembly that submits the convention proposition and the delegates shall be apportioned as is the House of Representatives. A Convention shall adopt no ordinance not necessary to the purpose for which the Convention has been called.

Section 2. Power to Revise or Amend Constitution Reserved to People

The people of this State reserve the power to amend this Constitution and to adopt a new or revised Constitution. This power may be exercised by either of the methods set out hereinafter in this Article, but in no other way.

Section 3. Revision or Amendment by Convention of the People

A Convention of the People of this State may be called pursuant to Section 1 of this Article to propose a new or revised Constitution or to propose amendments to this Constitution. Every new or revised Constitution and every constitutional amendment adopted by a Convention shall be submitted to the qualified voters of the State at the time and in the manner prescribed by the Convention. If a majority of the votes cast thereon are in favor of ratification of the new or revised Constitution or the constitutional amendment or amendments, it or they shall become effective January first next after ratification by the qualified voters unless a different effective date is prescribed by the Convention.

Section 4. Revision or Amendment by Legislative Initiation

A proposal of a new or revised Constitution or an amendment or amendments to this Constitution may be initiated by the General Assembly, but only if three-fifths of all the members of each house shall adopt an act submitting the proposal to the qualified voters of the State for their ratification or rejection. The proposal shall be submitted at the time and in the manner prescribed by the General Assembly. If a majority of the votes cast thereon are in favor of the proposed new or revised Constitution or constitutional amendment or amendments, it or they shall become effective January first next after ratification by the voters unless a different effective date is prescribed in the act submitting the proposal or proposals to the qualified voters.

ARTICLE XIV: MISCELLANEOUS

Section 1. Seat of Government

The permanent seat of government of this State shall be at the City of Raleigh.

Section 2. State Boundaries

The limits and boundaries of the State shall be and remain as they now are.

Section 3. General Laws Defined

Whenever the General Assembly is directed or authorized by this Constitution to enact general laws, or general laws uniformly applicable throughout the State, or general laws uniformly applicable in every county, city and town, and other unit of local government, or in every local court district, no special or local act shall be enacted concerning the subject matter directed or authorized to be accomplished by general or uniformly applicable laws, and every amendment or repeal of any law relating to such subject matter shall also be general and uniform in its effect throughout the State. General laws may be enacted for classes defined by population or other criteria. General laws uniformly applicable throughout the State shall be made applicable without classification or exception in every unit of local government of like kind, such as every county, or every city and town, but need not be made applicable in every unit of local government in the State. General laws uniformly applicable in every county, city and town, and other unit of local government, or in every local court district, shall be made applicable without classification or exception in every unit of local government, or in every local court district, as the case may be. The General Assembly may at any time repeal any special, local, or private act.

Section 4. Continuity of Laws; Protection of Office Holders

The laws of North Carolina not in conflict with this Constitution shall continue in force until lawfully altered. Except as otherwise specifically provided, the adoption of this Constitution shall not have the effect of vacating any office or term of office now filled or held by virtue of any election or appointment made under the prior Constitution of North Carolina and the laws of the State enacted pursuant thereto.

Section 5. Conservation of Natural Resources

It shall be the policy of this State to conserve and protect its lands and waters for the benefit of all its citizenry, and to this end it shall be a proper function of the State of North Carolina and its political subdivisions to acquire and preserve park, recreational, and scenic areas, to control and limit the pollution of our air and water, to control excessive noise, and in every other appropriate way to preserve as a part of the common heritage of this State its forests, wetlands, estuaries, beaches, historical sites, openlands, and places of beauty.
To accomplish the aforementioned public purposes, the State and its counties, cities and towns, and other units of local government may acquire by purchase or gift properties or interests in properties which shall, upon their special dedication to and acceptance by a law enacted by a vote of three-fifths of the members of each house of the General Assembly for those public purposes, constitute part of the 'State Nature and Historic Preserve,' and which shall not be used for other purposes except as authorized by law enacted by a vote of three-fifths of the members of each house of the General Assembly. The General Assembly shall prescribe by general law the conditions and procedures under which such properties or interests therein shall be dedicated for the aforementioned public purposes.

Section 6. Marriage

Marriage between one man and one woman is the only domestic legal union that shall be valid or recognized in this State. This section does not prohibit a private party from entering into contracts with another private party; nor does this section prohibit courts from adjudicating the rights of private parties pursuant to such contracts.

www.ingramcontent.com/pod-product-compliance
Lightning Source LLC
Chambersburg PA
CBHW052334220526
45472CB00001B/416